Other Books by Robert Abel Jr., MD

The Eye Care Revolution

The DHA Story

The One Earth Herbal Sourcebook

The Best Supplements for your Health

Lethal Hindsight

Last Sighting

Lumi's Book of Eyes

Lumi's Book of Teeth

Sheepdogs and Dragonflies

Is Death Really A Mystery?

PERSONAL STORIES
THAT LIFT THE VEIL

ROBERT ABEL JR., M.D.

Wasteland Press

www.wastelandpress.net
Shelbyville, KY USA

Is Death Really A Mystery?
Personal Stories that Lift the Veil
by Robert Abel Jr., MD

First Printing – January 2021
ISBN: 978-1-68111-376-0

Printed in the U.S.A.

0   1   2   3   4   5   6

For my wife, Mike:

Love you to the moon and back

"Heaven lies about us in our infancy
Shades of the prison-house begin to close
Upon the growing boy."

Excerpt from *Ode: Intimations of Immortality*
by William Wordsworth

(In other words, the child still sees what the adult has lost.)

TABLE OF CONTENTS

PROLOGUE

I was climbing up Maine's tallest mountain, Mount Katahdin, with my camp group and wanted to be the first one to get to the top.

Running ahead of the other kids most of the way, I came upon a deep crevasse that had to be jumped in order to continue. I was alone when I came upon a deep crevasse that brought me to a halt. I had to jump across it to continue on my path. It may have only been eighteen inches wide, but to my nine-year-old self it appeared extremely deep – frighteningly so. It took all of my courage to continue, but I took a deep breath, and a leap.

What I saw, in the second or two I hovered above the gap, I recall distinctly to this day. It was a spool of film that unraveled in a horizontal direction, and I immediately recognized that each little frame represented some piece of the story of my life.

Of course, the film moved too quickly for me to focus on any individual frame, but when I landed on the other side of the gap I knew the complete footage of my future life experiences existed; I had seen it in one, fleeting moment. And in that moment I innately understood the concept of déjà vu: that the 'past', 'present' and 'future' were linked and that a shift in my perspective allowed me to see parts that should have been invisible because they simply had not yet come into existence, or no longer existed.

CHAPTER ONE
Introduction

Sophocles, Aeschylus, Plato and Aristotle all debated the question of the soul and the afterlife. Egyptians had their sarcophagi and pyramids. The Romans and Greeks put their faith in the hands of their gods and even created visual images of eternal heaven and hell. European philosophers also struggled with the same questions

The hardwiring of the brain is geared for survival and limited to the five senses. Newton's, Einstein's, and Heisenberg's Laws may apply to electrons but cannot conceptualize how one's deceased spouse could walk into the bedroom, give a peck on the cheek, smile and then disappear into thin air.

This book is a compilation of ordinary people's encounters with death, dying and leaving their bodies. These stories provide insight into the fundamental quandary of our lives: why we are here and where we go after it all ends. These phenomena include memories, dreams, waking experiences and near-death events. The people who experience them, for the most part, are logical and rational, but have found that logic and rationality cannot explain the reality of that which is outside the physical being of this life.

Addressing and alleviating the fear of dying and death was the major reason for writing this book. The media has always exploited this fear because it commands attention and sells. The electronic media also highlights automobile deaths, opioid deaths, celebrity deaths, homicides, conflict fatalities, natural disasters, and is currently having a heyday with COVID-19. The daily COVID reports even introduce the death count before the number of people with infections.

How we address, suppress, or ignore the reality of death is deeply personal. But when a person crosses the threshold and returns or is visited by a loved one who has passed over, the event can be transformative. I have attempted to describe these experiences as they have been related to me, but how they affected or changed people is a much larger subject, worthy of a book in itself.

I have been privileged that so many people have shared their stories with me of their own accord. They have come to me as patients, colleagues, clergy, friends, or spontaneous acquaintances at social events. People might have spoken of their experiences because of a recent loss, chronic grieving or they are isolated. Some had never before shared their dream or awake sightings with anyone, even their closest relatives or confidants.

Why, then, did they tell me about their experiences? I suspect it's because, like me, they have always wondered what this mystery is all about. Although I trained as a medical doctor and follow science in my practice, I have never been able to dismiss near-death experiences and visitations as tricks of the mind. I have always been receptive to a new, unique report. Each one has been part of an exploration; a journey towards better understanding.

Whenever someone told me their story, I listened. With their permission, I wrote it down. I didn't stop to consider the impact these collected narratives could have on me. I certainly didn't anticipate sharing them with others. This intention developed during my own journey and exploration.

Along the way, I have had many experiences of my own, although I, too, rarely shared them with other people. I realized that dream events and altered states are difficult to understand and, very often, are reflexively rejected by logical people. Often, we do not know how to integrate these experiences into our daily lives. Since others may laugh at our story, ignore it completely, or just say 'that's nice', while stepping quickly away. It is natural to be hesitant about sharing extraordinary events outside of our control, even when they profoundly changed how we see the world and think about death.

People inherit many beliefs about dying and death from their families, background, education, or religious training. These preconceptions may not provide a foundation to make sense of the extraordinary experiences described in this book. Even when we have suffered the loss of someone close to us, we're conditioned to rely on information that arrives through the five senses and can be readily explained by observable phenomena. If someone receives information in a dream that would otherwise never have been discovered or is pronounced dead and returns to tell their tale, he or she often lacks the means to understand what has taken place. Relating it to another person is even more difficult to articulate. It is hard to comprehend or articulate experiences learned from childhood.

I am no more prepared than anyone else to declare that one experience is inherently different from any other. Each, to me, is an echo from an unseen network that binds all humans together, within and outside our physical self.

Despite their uniqueness and resistance to definition, I have found that these narratives have several common characteristics. Each time they were unsolicited, unanticipated, unexplained, and uncontrollable — yet they had meaning. They changed how the person thought about their world and whatever lies beyond it. I will share these conclusions in the final chapter.

While categorizing these experiences is a challenge, I believe that there is a framework or common threads that may arise from this exploration. This classification is an attempt to present these narratives as clearly as possible. I arbitrarily grouped these experiences into two main categories and seven subcategories.

The definitions I have used should help you consider the variety of experiences, but they should not detract from the actuality that they all are glimpses of a greater reality that our normal, waking mind cannot fathom.

Messages Coming to People from Beyond Themselves

- Dreams (Seeing)
- Dreams (Seeing and Hearing)
- Awake Encounters
- Symbolic Visitations
- Arousal from Coma

People Travelling Beyond Their Bodies

- Levitations
- Near-death experiences (NDEs)

How did I come to receive hundreds of narratives? I've explained how my job as a physician, and my own willingness to explore what science customarily leaves out, are factors. But I think the deeper reason is that connections between people, still living and beyond life, are real. All that is needed to see that web of connectivity is openness and acceptance. Healthy curiosity and inquisitiveness certainly help.

My conversations were almost always face to face. People perceived I was a good listener and concerned observer. One thing was for sure: People wanted to share these stories, because they were so powerful, or hard to understand. In most instances, the individual became very animated while reconnecting with the experience.

So, over the years, I recorded the most poignant and illustrative stories. It was only recently that I decided they were so numerous they had to be assembled into some type of compendium, which I could share with other people to break the taboo of death.

Those who shared their experiences were ordinary people from all walks of life. The majority were women. Only they, whether asleep or awake, in their bodies or removed, could understand the context of their experiences. It was only their interactions that I viewed as my responsibility to report.

The reported experiences are a small sample of the hundreds of stories that I have collected over the years. Each individual is identified by a pseudonym.

Whether the experiences came in dream or waking states, they are open to a great deal of interpretation. For that reason, I will not comment extensively on any particular story, and will only provide occasional observations to establish context or pose deeper questions. In the final chapters, I will share my own incidents and then reflect on the common threads that connect these accumulated testimonies.

CHAPTER TWO
Visitations While Asleep

VISIONS FROM BEYOND

The first set of stories combine what people have visualized and remembered from their dreams. The second set will feature what people have both seen and heard from the appearances in their dreams.

∞

Ninety-four-year-old Robert told me that he sees many different people in his dreams and stated, "I actually enjoy it!" He has been a widower for many years. "There is an uncertainty in my dreams about my wife," he confessed. "I know that she was there, but I do not have a lasting image. Maybe since we talked about this, I will see her tonight."

When I asked Robert about his dreams the next day, he said: "My wife appeared to me last night. It was not a complete scene, but I knew it was her. It was such a nice feeling…a nice thrill."

∞

Seventy-one-year-old Ed, a long-time friend and colleague, has shared several stories about seeing his father, a remarkable man in many ways, in his dreams. He was very close to his father, both personally and professionally, and worked with him for nearly thirty years, which accounted for so many memories. He stated, "In one such dream, we both attended a professional meeting together, watching a slideshow in full color. In another, I was sitting next to my father, who was wearing madras shorts and smoking a pipe, and we just had a grand old time without saying a word. I will never forget my father's twinkle in his eyes and his mischievous smile…and his love." Apparently, his father did not have to employ words to convey feelings.

Ed also related a vivid situational dream. "One day at the beach in Ocean City, Maryland, I was lost in the dune grass. Apparently, my family had walked off. I became increasingly frightened until someone from the beach patrol led me back to the center of the beach and my family returned."

Not all dreams are pleasant and reassuring. They can resurrect significant events from the past, in which we often feel a lack of control. Perhaps repeating an embedded event may somehow make it more conscious and even reduce the trauma.

∞

Ninety-four-year-old Juan shared a story about his dear wife, who had died four years prior to our conversation. "I saw her two or three months later. She was happy, and so I became happy. We had a special marriage, and she is always with me. It was so comforting." Like so many others, his memories of the visit were visually accurate and endured. He felt no appreciable difference between his dream and visits that occurred from living people in his waking life.

∞

A delightful seventy-four-year-old retired manager was eager to tell me the following story:

"My deceased husband appeared to me, looking around age twenty-two, with a cigarette hanging from his lip. He had actually stopped smoking in life thirty-five years ago. But on this occasion, he had the cigarette dangling from his lip, just like it would have when he was a very young man, with a twinkle in his eye. I got the message that he was alright."

∞

Maddie in her eighties told me, "I saw my dead grandson, walking in heaven. It was very brief but very profound. It sticks with me 'til this day."

∞

A lively fifty-one-year-old gentleman always had an upbeat attitude when I spent time with him. One day he decided to tell me about a dream that occurred the evening before. We had previously discussed the subject of dream encounters shortly after his father had passed. Perhaps he felt that the connection had been established.

"My parents appeared to me in a cloud. They were so happy. I couldn't believe it. It was so simple. After they smiled at me, they disappeared. It could not have been any longer than ten seconds, but it will leave me with a memory for a lifetime."

∞

Glenda, an 80-year-old friend, has a very positive attitude, but she has occasional moments of loneliness and solitude. In one such moment, she related to me, "I was sitting in my living room and staring at my dead husband's favorite chair. All of a sudden, I saw my husband in full detail, sitting in that chair for two seconds. It was over that quickly, but it touches my heart until this day. In another dream I heard him explicitly say, 'Why did that cost you so much?'"

Glenda also shared that she often feels his presence in her dreams.

∞

Eighty-eight-year-old Leann was cheerful except when there was any adversity in her family. She had lost a number of relatives, including her husband and her son.

On one visit, she shared with me that she had had a remarkable dream the previous night. "I saw my fifty-one-year-old disabled son, who appeared in the hallway, smiling at me. He was healthy and intact, and I knew he was in the right place."

She also shared with me that a few weeks after her husband's passing, he had appeared in a dream. This not only alleviated her grief but also gave her confidence that she had something to expect and prepare for after her own death.

∞

Eighty-five-year-old Fern visited me one morning so energized that I had to ask her what had happened. "My son died many years ago," she stated. "Many times, he's visited me in my dreams, always just smiling. He showed up again last night. Like always, he didn't say anything, but it made me so happy. Perhaps this is due to my need for reinforcement about knowing he was okay, so I could be too."

∞

Seventy-eight-year-old Jenny said her recently deceased husband visited her three times in two weeks. "He came again last night," she once told me. "He is always looking younger and healthy. Nothing was said, but it was felt. We enjoyed our time together, and perhaps I just needed more shared time together."

∞

Seventy-eight-year-old Vicki told me that she has seen lots of deceased people in her family numerous times in her dreams. However, she had only visualized her son just once, immediately after his death. "Why only once?" she asked. "Perhaps his one visit was just to reassure me that he is well in his world, and that was enough to quell my pain."

∞

Fifty-two-year-old Linda told me, "I saw my deceased relative on the beach many times. It became obvious to me that he was my soulmate." She did not elaborate on the relationship, but she seemed quite content and was grateful to share.

∞

Seventy-three-year-old Dina frequently sees her father whenever she is stressed. She stated that he always looks young and healthy but doesn't ever speak.

When talking about it, she emphasized, "These are real observations." As if I would not believe her and think otherwise.

∞

Ninety-one-year-old Ned told me, "My fourth son returns spontaneously whenever I ask to see him." He stated that his parents do not frequently visit him, but he accepted that he has no control over that situation and may have a much closer bond his son.

∞

A sixty-five-year-old Indian woman, Dhala, shared with me that she frequently sees her dead mother in dreams. She apparently was very close to her mother and the visits mean a lot to her. She associated these dreams with times in which she has needed additional support. She explained that she was not very close to her father. "He did not return often."

It may be our closest friends and relatives that are most likely to engage, message, and comfort us. This is how I explain the recurring visits from my parents. I can only wonder how many more people who have had these experiences have not shared them.

∞

Eighty-eight-year-old Brie told me an interesting story. "My deceased husband walked up the cellar steps. I knew this was a dream, but he looked good, appeared to be younger, and smiled. He didn't have to say anything; he made me feel good. I also saw my father just walking by after he died."

∞

A retired woman told me, "I had a dream on my birthday last year. I was bedridden and not feeling well. In my dream, I saw my mother, who often had been a very unhappy person. She appeared to be very religious in the dream. In this instance, she was very happy and smiled at me. Seeing her made me feel instantly better and very happy, too. I immediately began to cry tears of joy; I normally do not cry at all. I was so happy to see that my mother was so joyful. She also told me, 'Get up, get out of bed, and get some air'." Could her mother be joyful because she has been relieved from her burdens in life in her present state? Or perhaps because she found it easier in this manifestation to connect with and care for her daughter?

∞

Forty-five-year-old Warren has an aggressive cancer and is on three chemotherapies and concurrent radiation. He has been through all kinds of therapies, is in a very worried and haggard state and has lost a lot of weight.

When he mentioned dreams, he stated, "My father and uncle (both deceased) are chasing me in a dream. It is not for me to interpret whatever they want from me. Maybe they are just trying to keep me alive."

∞

Fifty-two-year-old Hu, who is Chinese-American, has seen both of her parents on multiple occasions. "My father died in 2005. My mother died later. Both came to me several times in dreams." She smiled as she made these recollections.

∞

Twenty-seven-year-old Ted visited me to assist with some household chores. For no reason, we engaged in a very personal conversation regarding missing important people in our lives. He told me that he had been extremely close to his maternal grandparents who had passed years before. "I have seen each of them multiple times in dreams, and it was quite reassuring. And my mom had had even more sightings."

∞

Seventy-six-year-old Bill had lost both his oldest daughter and his wife.

"My wife passed away four years ago, and I frequently see her smiling at me in my dreams. She used to make fun of me because my real name was not William. She loved to joke around that way.

"Once I heard her footsteps walking down the stairs, so I jumped out of bed and ran to the stairwell. Nobody was there. I could only smile because I knew it was her.

"My oldest daughter was killed in an automobile accident just after her high school graduation. She was the prettiest thing and always happy-go-lucky. She brought joy to everyone she met. She lit up the room. Well, I see her smile all the time in dreams, and it makes me happy for a while."

MESSAGE FROM BEYOND

I have known an eighty-eight-year-old grand dame, Thelma, for a longtime. She was a very rational person who did not believe in heaven or an afterlife. But on one occasion she said, "I have to tell you something. Last night, my father came to me in a dream and told me about the lost heirloom ring. It was in an overlooked slip in a closet. I popped up at two in the morning, went to the chest of drawers in the closet, looked in a little pocket on the silk slip, and there it was! This ring had been my mother's, her mother's, and maybe even someone's before that. I was overjoyed, both seeing and hearing my father and retrieving the ring."

∞

A fifty-eight-year-old chef, Aimee, had numerous unexplained experiences in her life, the first of which, she told me, concerned money, often a source of worry for her. She was working two jobs to make ends meet.

"One night in a dream, I saw my mother and heard her tell me where the fifty dollars was," she told me. "It was lost in the bedroom, underneath a cabinet. The next morning, I got up and looked there, and lo and behold, it was just where Mother said it would be! I was happy for both the money and for seeing my dear mom."

∞

Heather, in her sixties, has had even more unusual experiences. After Christmas dinner one year, she was cleaning up the dishes for the entire family and her three-year-old grandson kept nagging at her to drag him in the new little red wagon that she had purchased for him. He finally put his hands on his hips, looked at her and stated, "I pulled you in a little red wagon when you were my grandchild!" Out of the mouth of babes, Wordsworth might say.

Heather had many curious interactions with this grandson. Once, the grandson was traveling from Florida with Heather's son and daughter-in-law. South of Washington D.C., they stopped at a telephone station to call. "Mom," the daughter-in-law said, "we are two and a half hours away from home, and we will be home for dinner."

Heather recalled the incident this way: "My grandson grabbed the phone and said, 'No, we won't. We are going to have a flat tire over the bridge, and we won't be there until after dinner.'" Which, as it turned out, was exactly what happened."

Her grandson would be a grown man by now. Maybe he became a stockbroker, since he seemed to know things in advance. Likelier, like most of us, he lost that ability with age.

∞

An eleven-year-old child who came into my office with her mother shared two experiences with me that had occurred several years earlier. When she was around eight, she was missing a favorite ring. In a dream, her great-grandmother came to her and informed her it lay behind a drawer in a desk. The next morning, she got up, removed the drawer, and found the ring. Needless to say, she was delighted.

Several years earlier, the same great-grandmother had appeared to the girl as a hologram, in which only the woman's face and neck were visible. Her lips did not move. She said, "I am leaving now. Please tell the family I love them." The great-grandmother spoke two languages, neither of which was English, and the child at that time spoke only English.

It is just one example of communication occurring without speech or movement of the lips, and through a medium that transcends any language or dialect.

∞

A sixty-year-old friend decided to share with me a deeply important dream. "This is the most memorable dream about my dad that came to me months after his death," she said. "My mother had been getting more and more upset about how his mission work was being changed from the way our father had run the place. Dad came to me in a dream and told me, 'It is not my mission anymore. Don't let it upset you.' From then on, my mother and I found peace about things."

"One other little thing," she continued. "We believe in God. My dad passed quickly. We had no idea he was sick but on the day my dad passed, the day's title of the devotional we read was *Transformed*. I would think that my dad had shared with you that he had been an alcoholic in his early days, living off the street. As he would say, accepting Jesus Christ as his Savior, he was transformed. He repeated this story so often. His favorite church song was *Transformed*. The night of his death, my mom, my sister, and I heard that same song in the very same dream. It gave us peace and made us feel that it was God's plan that Dad would pass away that day."

∞

A thirty-seven-year-old Pakistani woman, Nada, often had seen her parents after their deaths. During their lives, she was particularly close to her father. On numerous occasions, she stated, "My father has come to me in dreams to give me advice, especially about one of my six children, a son who was born deaf and blind. The discussions seem extremely real." She recalled them with ease and described them vividly.

This particular son, now a young man in his twenties. Coming to America, he could neither see nor hear. He ultimately received bilateral cataract surgery for his vision and cochlear ear implants to improve his hearing. Although his speech is incomplete, he can now communicate vigorously and began enjoying some essential things he missed in adolescence, like playing games, watching television, and being a contributing family member.

∞

Ninety-one-year-old Tessie told me, "In 2007, my husband died. One week later, he appeared to me in a dream with all seven of our deceased dogs and said, 'We are all doing well.'"

"Arthur," she had said. "What took you so long?" He stated that he had to find her before he could appear.

Tessie told me her niece had seen her Uncle Arthur on the night that he died, but had not shared her story until Tessie opened up about her own experience. She went on to share two other important dreams with the niece.

Tessie also shared that she had three mothers growing up. One was her biological mother and the other two were her older sisters. The two sisters were one year apart and they doted on her. Needless to say, she was very close to them.

"Several times in dreams, my two sisters appeared together, smiled, and shared some thoughts with me. It was very pleasant and supportive, and they looked so young and happy together." After Tessie's father died, she said, he also made an appearance in one of her dreams. "My father appeared in the darkness, whereas my mother appeared in a lovely breeze. And furthermore, my niece was first notified of her husband's death when he came to her in a dream and told her!"

∞

Victor, a sixty-five-year-old Puerto Rican man, told me a story that related to him in a personal and professional fashion. "I have taken over my deceased father's cleaning business. Frequently, my father comes to me in dreams and gives me business advice. Don't you know it, he is often correct!"

∞

Ninety-two-year-old Charles told me, "My wife walked through the door and said that she loved me. It changed the way I grieved. It has been several years since my wife passed away and every once in a while, I get a hint that she has popped back because of something said by another person. For instance, I was sitting at the dining room table, facing the doorway. My neighbor walked in and the sun at her back cast a light around her while dimming her features. I said, 'You're back!' Although it was only the neighbor, it was exhilarating."

∞

Ninety-seven-year-old Enid volunteered that she had seen her deceased husband and been relieved. She chuckled when she said "So many times, whenever I had to make a big decision, he popped into my mind or into my dreams. He would call me 'Tootsie'. He would give me some kind of signal." She told me this with a big smile on her face.

∞

Eighty-five-year-old woman's husband died recently. She shared this story. "He came to tell me and he was very well and younger. I have seen my mother many times, but this is the first and only time I saw my husband. It appears that I have the capacity to have multiple sightings. Dreams make me feel so much better being alone."

∞

One morning, SP decided to ask her deceased mother, who had been a nurse, to provide her with some help. "I asked for help with my son who was having a significant medical condition. Sixteen years after her death, I had never seen my mother or heard from her. However, at 2:14 a.m. on the morning after, I heard my mother yell, 'SP, you can figure it out!' Needless to say, I sat bolt upright. I had waited sixteen years for a connection."

∞

At ninety-three, Nora had been a widow several times and always seemed doubtful about any conversation about people appearing in dreams. She was kind and generous and would smile if her friends' conversation turned to that particular subject, but she would never participate. Then at dinner one evening, she pulled me aside and wanted to share with me a particular moment.

Several nights before, she had had a dream in which she and a dear friend, who had been deceased for several months, were together for an afternoon. They both knew it was a dream and that the decreased woman indeed was dead, but it seemed so real and so energizing. Before the deceased lady departed, she wanted to thank Nora for being so kind to her daughter. When the dream ended, Nora was left with a feeling of strong attachment, comfort, and goodness.

Approximately a year later, Nora had her second vivid dream. "I was traveling down an escalator when a deceased relative was moving upwards on the adjacent escalator. Just as we were smiling and passing each other, a nondescript individual grabbed her pocketbook and ran up the escalator. It turned out that the purse-snatching had actually happened, and I was amazed to be able to recapture it in minute detail."

∞

Carla is a very intelligent woman in her late sixties who has traveled frequently for her personal and family businesses. She related the following dreams to me:

"My son Edward was a frail, asthmatic child of seven when we visited a dude ranch in the hill country just north of San Antonio. The first night we were there, I awoke at 4:00 a.m. after dreaming that he had been stung by a scorpion as he stood in the bathroom barefoot. The dream was extremely vivid, showing precisely which tile the scorpion was located on and playing the pitter patter of Edward's bare feet as he ran across that tile. Then it showed me the horror of his death in the medical evacuation helicopter that came to take him to the hospital. He died in the dream.

"At 5:00 a.m., I was still trying to force myself to go back to sleep, believing that I was just being a typical overprotective mother. Then I had a strong feeling that I was really needed. So, I went into the bathroom and spotted the scorpion on the very tile where I had seen it. While grabbing a shoe to kill it, I heard the pitter patter of my son's feet as he ran towards the bathroom.

"I was aghast, then relieved, and then emotionally drained. But from this experience, I gained confidence in my insight and ability to understand messages from dreams.

"Another time I dreamed I was to cancel my 10:00 a.m. dental appointment in the morning and expect a call from my ex-husband at that specific time. The message was that if I was not home to receive the call, he would not call another time.

"When I awoke, I called the dentist's office, paid the late cancellation fee with a credit card, and waited for my phone call. At three minutes after 10:00 a.m., Fred called and offered me an increase in child support. It was exactly what I was told I would receive in my dream. He continued to pay that for approximately ten months, giving me an opportunity to start a small business. After that, I was able to start two separate businesses, which allowed me to raise my children comfortably."

∞

A thirty-two-year-old female technician happily shared a unique experience. "Ten years ago, my deceased mother appeared in a dream and said, 'I have never been so happy.' I didn't require any further evidence to know that she was safe and happy and that she was in a good place."

∞

Seventy-three-year-old Barney told me about his best friend growing up. "He was more like a brother. I knew him all my life. My father died when I was only seven, but my good friend always remembered him, and it warmed my heart. We did all kinds of things together in the neighborhood. He died after a short illness, and I was really shaken up. After several days, things settled down and in a dream, he appeared to me and seemed to share some information. In fact, he said, 'Thank you for everything.' He looked thirty years old and was very healthy. Really, he was more like a brother than a best friend."

∞

A retired psychologist attended a memorial service held one year after the passing of sixty-nine year old Ruth's father. After the service, as the people were chatting in the lobby,

MG, the deceased man's daughter, volunteered this sentinel interaction with the group of attendees.

Ruth volunteered, 'I had a dream last night in which my father came to me and very clearly said, 'Why haven't you called me?'

I responded, 'Because you are dead.'

He replied, 'You still can call me!'

And then he vanished."

This is one of only a few stories I have been told in which the image of the deceased gives this specific instruction as an introduction. Many people have told me about receiving commands to perform some type of service, or suggestions for how to act. This stands as a direct request to initiate conversation.

CHAPTER THREE
Visitations While Awake

Many visitations appear when people are awake, but may be so fleeting or in the peripheral vision, they are unrecognized. This is not the case for the following stories in this chapter. These individuals have seen, heard, felt and, even one case, smelled the presence of their deceased loved ones. These evocative stories are a clue to contemporary realities.

∞

Sixty-five-year-old Leslie remembered a day from earlier in her life, when she had been changing her baby's diaper. She felt a presence on her left side. She was very specific about that position. "When I finally turned around to the left, I saw my deceased father walking out the door and immediately ran after him, with a baby in hand. He turned around, smiled, and then disappeared."

∞

Sixty-five-year-old thoracic surgeon, Art, had worked on the front line in Vietnam and was used to treating critical wounds in both Americans and Vietnamese prisoners. On one particular day, he told me, "They brought in a wounded and dying North Vietnamese soldier. He had 90% body burns, which meant that he was not going to survive, and he was suffering greatly."

Art suspected the soldier did not want to live in extreme agony. "I decided to help him out of his misery, since there was no other option, and gave him a lethal dose of intravenous morphine. That night, as I pulled down my bedcovers and was ready to climb into my cot, I saw this man's face, wearing his cap with the red star, appear in front of me. The hologram image said, 'I want to thank you for your kindness.' I have never had a significant dream like that again."

∞

Clyde, a general surgeon, had a recurrent waking visitation that he shared with me about his father, who was also a physician. "When I have a quandary about a patient who I have examined, I feel my father telling me what the appropriate action should be. I accept it and suddenly know that it is the correct option, and it works!"

∞

Terry, a forty-seven -year-old woman, lost her son because of drowning. One night when she was getting under the covers while her husband was already asleep in the bed, she saw her son walk out of the water directly in front of her, and come up to the bedside and say, 'Mom, I am alright.' He then disappeared. She felt uncomfortable mentioning this experience to her family at that time, and only discussed with me.

∞

Jim had lost his wife very suddenly three years previously. When he revealed this to me, I asked if he had seen her.

"Why do you ask?" he responded.

I said that I find that people occasionally have some sort of story to tell and sometimes it is actually very soothing to share it with another person. He took off his glasses, rubbed his eyes, and suppressed a tear.

"I was massaging my temples two nights ago before going to sleep. I saw black, and then my vision turned blue, and my wife's face appeared like a hologram and she stated,

'It is so wonderful here; you will like it. I love you.' She then disappeared."

∞

Norman, eighty-four years old, had lost his dear wife after fifty-four years of marriage. "My wife Kathleen passed away August 27, 2013 at 2:21 a.m. I miss her as though she had died five minutes ago. A month or less after she died, I had a vivid dream. She was with me, approximately two or three feet in front of me, wearing a plain light blue nightgown with very short sleeves. It was neck-high and came to her feet. She was barefoot. She came to me and put her arms around me, laid her head on my shoulder, and said clearly, 'I don't feel good'. And then she disappeared."

He could not understand the visit or the discomfort she described. In the stories I've collected, a loved one in discomfort appears much less frequently than one bearing a positive greeting.

Norman shared other experiences he called "miracles", which occurred periodically. The first came while changing a battery for a garage door opener. He couldn't dislodge the fourth screw. He shaved down the Phillips-head screwdriver and could still not move the screw. He was working up a sweat and getting impatient.

"I finally walked away to get a drink and while doing so, I looked up and said, 'Kathleen, please help me out on this one!' A few minutes later, not one to give up, I applied myself to the task but to my surprise, that final screw had raised itself a sixteenth of an inch from where it was and was easily removed.

"In the underground garage of my apartment house, there are only four reserved handicapped parking spaces. Each time I approached, as the garage door went up, I would say, 'Kathleen, please save me a good spot…and she does."

Norman and his wife must have had quite a close relationship. Either that, or he's mastered the power of positive thinking.

∞

Fifty-five-year-old Marcie was very close to her family in South America. She shared the following experience.

A number of years ago, the night that her mother died, she visualized her sitting at the bottom of the stairway in her house. Some of her cousins were sitting higher up on the steps in white outfits, like angels. In the dream, she rushed over to her mother and embraced her for a long time, until her mother said, "I have to go now."

"It was like my mother knew that I needed some consolation. On multiple other occasions, when I'm drained, my mother appears to provide solace. This indicates to me that there is some continuity to life."

More recently, Marcie told me there had been serious complications in her life, but that she had been in denial. One night, she was lying in bed when suddenly her mother appeared next to her, on the right side. Her mother put on a stern face, clapped her hands as a warning, and stomped her foot. Clapping the hands, in Marcie's family, is a symbol to wake up or "get to it". Her mother called her by name but did not say anything else. However, Marcie understood exactly what the warning was about, and why her mother wanted her to wake up and get out of denial. After this moment, her deceased mom smiled and disappeared.

∞

Eighty-seven-year-old Selma shared two experiences. "I went to church at six in the morning after an argument with my husband," she told me. "While I was sitting in the second row, a bearded man shuffled up the aisle, stopped alongside of me, and said, 'I have a prayer for you.' He gave me the prayer, walked away, and disappeared halfway down the aisle.

"A bit later, the priest read the very same prayer. I felt refreshed and was no longer angry with my husband. It also was interesting because I am always afraid to go places alone, including church, but this time I left church feeling happy and fulfilled."

Selma's husband happened to die sometime later that same year. "Three months later, I experienced something very unusual and frightening. I had just moved and was living alone in a small apartment. I frequently became anxious and often a little depressed since my husband had passed. I was lying in bed one night and noticed that the light was on under the bathroom door. I was certain that I had turned it off. I cowered under the covers. The door then opened, and out walked my husband. He proceeded to get into the bed, and I felt his warm body next to me. This lasted for thirty seconds, and then he got out of bed and walked out the door.

"I was amazed, but again, I felt refreshed. My feelings of mourning and grief began to recede."

∞

Some memories are about people that may be closer to another person in the family.

Edgar is a seventy-two-year-old professional who had a remarkable encounter in the most ordinary circumstances. "I was shaving and looking in the mirror. The door to the bathroom was closed. The door then opened, and I saw this image going down the stairs. I ran out into the hallway and looked down the stairs. There was a man, still going down the stairs and whistling. I knew that my wife doesn't whistle so after the man disappeared and I finished shaving, I came downstairs to my wife and told her the story. She stared at me without understanding and thought that I had made up the story. So, I whistled the melody to her, and she immediately began crying. She knew who it was that I had heard and seen. It was her deceased father."

∞

Paula, an eighty-two-year-old widow, told me one of the more unusual stories I have encountered. She awoke most days at 7:00 a.m. like clockwork. However, on one particular morning, she awoke at 3:00 a.m.

"I could not go back to sleep, so I went downstairs," she told me. "I saw my deceased husband sitting at the head of the dining room table, smiling at me. It was remarkable! He said, 'I love you' and disappeared.

"I was unable to go back to sleep, so I tinkered around the kitchen until the phone rang at 6:30. It was my son from Baltimore. 'Mom,' he said, 'you won't believe whom I saw at 3:00 this morning.'"

I have not heard of another instance in which two people were visited simultaneously, in different locations, by the same deceased loved one.

∞

Bella, a thirty-two-year-old woman, shared with me what she felt was a miraculous experience about her deceased husband. "A few months ago, while I was awake, my husband got in bed with me. It was such an unexpected and joyous occurrence that I wanted it to last forever. However, his presence soon faded but left the lasting impression that it was real. It will be always remembered."

∞

A 92-year-old woman not only sees her deceased husband at night but also occasionally gets to physically feel him by her side. "He comes and gets under the covers with me. Sometimes we just lie in bed and sometimes he is under the comforter and pulls the quilt up over his head like he used to do, pulling it off of my side. His touching is endearing but he never says a word. I get up, go to the bathroom, and he is gone. Occasionally, he walks into the bathroom in his underwear, or less. It is amazing. It must be a tribute to our closeness for sixty-five years."

∞

Marty is a sixty-year-old professional who lived in the same town as his mother, who at eighty insisted that she really wanted to die. He got a new Newfoundland dog who immediately bonded with his mother, but her only response was, "At least the dog will make you happy."

Six days later, he was taking his mother out to dinner and put her in the passenger seat of the car. When he walked around to the other side and opened the door, he found her not breathing. A few minutes later, she was pronounced dead and was taken to a hospital.

She had arranged to donate her body to science, which was sent to a near-by medical school. Marty said, with irony, "I felt that my mother was disappointed not to have a doctor in the family. At least somebody got into medical school in the family."

Three years later, he got a call from the medical center that they had completed the study of the body and it was going to be cremated and could be sent to a cemetery or a mortuary. He felt that it should be sent to New Jersey, where she had been born. He hand-picked the urn for her ashes, but did nothing with them.

Two months later, she appeared at the foot of the bed. "Marty!" she said. "God damn it! You should bury me. Get off your butt and get me buried."

One month later, he popped up out of a dream in which he had seen her again and been told that he had been left enough money to have her buried. She stated that she didn't want to be on a shelf in an urn forever. Marty procrastinated for several more weeks and finally asked his sister to resolve the situation.

The sister went to Atlantic City, threw the ashes up in the air, and they took to the wind. Shortly thereafter, hurricane Sandy descended on the New Jersey shoreline and churned up the sand, sea and air. As it happened, Marty's mother's request had been to spread her ashes over her favorite beaches. He has not seen his mother since.

∞

Thirty-six-year-old Norene recounted two stories she found unforgettable, as did I. They both involved her young children, although Norene witnessed both events.

At age three, her son picked up the telephone while they were in a hotel room in Colombia, getting ready for a family wedding. He started talking to someone, even though the telephone had never rung. "Who are you talking to?" Norene asked.

"It is Ita. She said that everything is going to be okay."

Norene was taken aback. The child's deceased grandmother did not speak English and her son did not speak Spanish.

Three years later, Norene's eighteen-month-old daughter was looking up from her crib and waving both hands.

"Who are you waving at?" Norene asked the infant.

"Ita, Ita!"

Interestingly, neither child had ever met or seen this grandmother. Yet, these children clearly engaged with Ita and understood a message she conveyed. They understood a type of communication without a common language. These stories harken to Wordsworth's Intimations of Immortality, in which the poet affirms that young children retain the ability to see beyond our material world.

∞

Ninety-two-year-old Bernice was taking her stockings off in the bedroom. She described what came next as a most delightful experience. "I saw my deceased husband enter the room. He gave me a kiss on the cheek and said, 'See you later' and walked out." She was so pleased and reassured that he was happy and somewhere nice. A month later, Bernice also passed.

∞

Sixty-year-old Lois and her mother always had been extremely close. When Lois shared with me that her mother had died, I expressed my condolences and said that I hoped that she was in a better place.

Lois responded, "I know she is,"

"How do you know that?" I responded.

"I was in church last Sunday. I was sitting in a pew and I saw her walk up the aisle towards me. She put a kiss on my lips. She smiled and then disappeared. From the kiss, I knew it was her, and that she was happy."

Just telling the story made Lois cheerful and full of smiles. It's an energy I have seen in many people who told similar stories.

∞

Hank, a widower for several months, shared that while he was awake, his wife continuously followed him. He reported that "It was the strangest thing. Her eyes occasionally follow me when I am in the kitchen. I knew she was dead, but her face and eyes would suddenly appear. At other times, she would walk around from the stove over to the sink, but she always kept looking directly at me. This didn't occur often, but it is quite comforting."

∞

Enid's mother died a number of years ago. She shared, "After dying, my mother followed me all around the house for a day. Then the following day, she disappeared. She always thought that I not only was the symbol of intelligence, but also of death. Perhaps this is because, I am a pastor and have officiated at a many funerals and memorial services."

∞

Ninety-one-year-old Lee was sound asleep one night when she heard her recently deceased husband call out her name, plain as day.

"I woke right up and saw him standing there in front of me. He smiled and then disappeared. Another time, I was watching TV when my husband appeared to be standing in the study. He called my name. I believe he came back to see if I was okay."

Lee told me she had lost her son five years ago. She still wonders why he hasn't paid a visit.

∞

Eighty-six-year-old Meg's husband had died six years previously. Since his passing she has had multiple dream state and waking connections with him.

The first occurred on the night of his funeral. She was lying in bed and thinking about him when he appeared at the foot of the bed. He said, "I told you, hon, that I would come back and I would never leave you."

She bolted upright, jumped out of bed, went to hug him and fell flat on her face. He had gone.

Meg has made a habit of talking to him during waking hours and touches the urn that contains his ashes at night. Besides visits in her recurring dreams, he once appeared when she was awake to inquire "What did you do with my black boots?"

"I had them resoled." she answered. "Then he disappeared."

However, at other times when I am watching television, his face will flash in front of me, out of the blue. I feel that he is always with me and continues to watch over me." She cheerfully told me that she shared the best years of her life with him.

I believe in her heart she feels her time with him has continued just in a new dynamic. This helps mitigate her pain and loneliness and, conversely, allows her to be strong as she explores a new phase of her life.

∞

Fifty-four-year-old Teddie was very close to her mother. "My mom was a small, highly energetic lady who was full of life until the year before she got sick, and died," she told me. "That was five years ago, and I have hoped to see her somehow in my dreams because I've heard lots of stories. However, I've had frequent contacts with my mother because I could smell her favorite perfume, Emeraude. When I would smell that aroma, especially when I was having some kind of stress in my life, and I would know that she was there.

"Once, when my husband was nearby, I asked him if he smelled anything. And he said he didn't. So, obviously only I received these messages. But from this sensation of her presence, I always became more reassured."

CHAPTER FOUR

Symbolic Visitations

These extraordinary experiences seem to require people to be in a certain frame of mind to perceive them. The right mood, meditative state, relaxed attitude, or just being temporarily free from multitasking may allow the portal to open.

In the dreams described in this section, the visitation does not feature a relative or even a person. The central image perceived is usually a symbol that would have meaning only to the observer. Often these perceptions take the form of animals, but they can be representations of meaningful situations that occur at a later date.

∞

A gentleman shared that his seventy-seven-year-old wife died after a respiratory arrest. On what would have been her next birthday, her picture fell off the wall in front him and all of their children. He said "She always wanted to create a big splash on her birthday. This was just like her."

∞

One night, months after eighty-eight-year-old Gloria's husband passed, she was surprised to see him appear in a dream. Her initial response was to admonish him by saying "You have not been here to advise me when you were needed". He didn't respond and disappeared in an instant.

The next morning, she found two Luden's cough drops in the dishwasher. "Whenever there is an issue, like last night, I find Luden's cough drops, which he always had in his pocket."

Gloria decided to go to Marshall's and buy a new coat. "I found a nice, warm red coat I liked, took it off the rack, and put my hands in the pockets," she told me. "In one of the pockets were three Luden's cough drops."

She also shared that while asleep one night, her husband appeared to her. "How is it there?" she enquired.

"Like this, but much better." That remark was very encouraging to her. Her husband's visitations continue to comfort her.

∞

A friend's mother died and returned to her in dreams in two different forms. sixty-five-year-old Elaine told me that two nights after her mother's passing, she appeared in a dream wearing a nightgown but with an unlined, much younger face.

"Did you get your new body yet?" Elaine asked her mom.

"Not yet, but it will be soon."

Shortly thereafter, in one of Elaine's dreams a tiny owl was perched on her finger, accompanying her through a whole afternoon. She interpreted this as an introduction to her mother's 'new body'.

∞

Before a dear friend of my wife died, she informed her closest friends that she would try to give them a message after she passed. Within days, her next-door neighbor told me, "The lights would come on in my house for no reason. I would turn them off, and they would come on again. I knew it was her. She was my neighbor and we were best of friends."

This exact same phenomenon occurred to my wife, who experienced the flickering of bedroom lights on two separate occasions. She concluded that this was the very same deceased woman thanking her for willingness to look after her children.

∞

A doctor of my acquaintance is known as an extremely sensitive, compassionate individual as well as an excellent physician. When a person who worked in his practice — a highly respected and valued employee — was diagnosed with terminal cancer, he made time to visit her several times each week. One night he had this sentinel dream:

"I was walking into a very large room. Three sides of the room were lined with upright caskets. Many were Egyptian sarcophaguses. They were designed so that if someone walked into one of the caskets sideways and then turned horizontally, they would be able to remain restrained without falling out. I remembered the dream vividly and recognized that it was going to happen soon for my friend and colleague." Shortly thereafter she passed.

I feel dreams can be premonitions. The feelings we experience can be joyous or dreadful, depending on the context of the circumstances and timing of the dream. In other cases, the dreamer simply accepts the mood or message that pervades the experience.

∞

Sixty-one-year-old Cindy, a very dear friend, is a very private person. I have been privileged to hear accounts of her experiences, which she does not share with others.

She has found that her dreams may herald a loved one's passing, or an important event in a person's life. She dreamed of the passing of her grandmother, her uncle, and her cousins. "Each time a certain white dove would appear, and I knew what it was and who it represented," she told me.

In another dream, the appearance of a dove coincided with a friend's father dying from COVID-19 complications. In this case, she did not immediately realize what was happening; she found out the next day when her friend called to inform her of the man's passing.

Cindy has a close friend whose father never recovered completely from an auto accident. Although she never knew it, he developed a urinary tract infection and sepsis. She saw the man vividly in a dream during the night he passed. Similarly, she had a whole night of dreams about a couple who were anticipating the death of a relative. That death occurred, Cindy told me, during the same night she dreamed about the couple.

∞

Forty-five-year-old Kevin reported that he had visualized both his mother and father leave their bodies at the time of their deaths. He stated "I was amazed to observe them cross over. They went upwards like smoke into the light. This gave me some consolation for each loss and assuaged my own fear of death."

∞

Seventy-six-year-old Harriet's mother loved hummingbirds. "Within a month after my mother died, a hummingbird appeared, and for at least sixty seconds and it stared at me through the window. Later it appeared again, flew right in front of my face, and stared at me for another twenty seconds."

Harriet, a very compassionate social worker, had an unforgettable experience that occurred after she returned from work one day at about 6:00 p.m. She was resting in an easy chair and looking out the window. Suddenly, one of her clients, who had been very ill, appeared in front of her and said, "Thank you, Harriet. I am going." She fully understood that her client had just passed, and later confirmed the incident had occurred near the time of her experience.

∞

"My mother loved cardinals," sixty-two Penny told me. "For a year after she died, a cardinal came to our windowsill off and on. I knew what that meant and who it represented."

∞

Septuagenarian Cheryl shared with me that her husband had died eleven months previously and that she missed him terribly. She had no experience of him for several months after his passing, until one otherwise ordinary day. "I was sitting alone in the dining room, looking at a 'viney' plant adjacent to the cellar door. The plant started waving furiously for fifteen seconds and stopped. It waved again for another time.

"My husband loved that plant. There was no wind, no open door, nothing else happening, and no one else was in the house. So, I guess he was giving me a message."

Two weeks prior to visiting me, Cheryl had a unique experience: "A fly would come out and would land on my television set and stare at me. It was a cold November, and not the season for flies. My husband never wanted to hurt an animal, even a fly. He was upset that I would try to swat flies. This fly came out only when I was watching television, between 8:00 and 11:00 p.m. and continued to stare at me. I felt it was him, making his presence felt!"

∞

Forty-two-year-old Lisa's mother loved roses and doted on them every June when they bloomed. After her death, in mid-January, a rose bush in Lisa's yard bloomed in full. This recurred several times in consecutive years. She felt that Mom was just saying "hello."

∞

After seventy-year-old Millie's husband died, he returned to deliver a very specific instruction. "I saw and heard my husband clearly in a dream at which time he told me to go upstairs into the attic at my grand-uncle's house and open his trunk," Millie told me. "I did, and I found a picture of my grand-uncle in uniform on a postcard, a carte de physique. I was shocked! It was the spitting image of my deceased husband, Walter. I still cannot get over that."

∞

The next two stories are provided by individuals who experienced dreams which feature historical settings. Both men share characteristics which correlate with their visitations.

Many years ago, I spoke with the son of a friend, WL, a 45-year-old tradesman in Virginia. His family were outdoors people, and his father was a wildlife protector in a national reserve.

The males of his family were usually hunters, but WL had never touched a gun. He told me, "One night I had a vivid dream in color. I was a German soldier in battle and was killed; the images kept flashing the year 1943. I recognized the situation while in my dream. When I awoke, I realized why I would never shoot anything. Therefore, I could never go hunting with my family or friends or even touch a gun."

∞

During a routine eye exam, I asked Candace how her sleep had been in case the blue light from the television was disturbing it. She replied that she had not slept well in the last two months since the death of her beloved husband. She then volunteered the following narrative:

"I visited my husband daily in his hospital room. On one particular day I did not see the regular day nurse. In her place was a lovely young nurse named Angel. She was soft spoken and updated me on my husband's declining medical status. Then she touched my elbow and asked if he were to have a cardiac arrest should he be resuscitated. I said no, let him finally be in peace. She put her arm around me and said, 'You made the correct decision. You will be alright.'

"That night my husband did, in fact, pass. I came in the next morning to collect his belongings. I met the regular day nurse and thanked her for her care and compassion. I then went out to the nurses' station and asked for Angel so that I could thank her, as well. The clerk informed me that there was no nurse named Angel on the floor, nor was there ever someone by that name. Confused, I looked anxiously to find my husband's doctor. When I put the question to him, he confirmed that there had never been an Angel on his floor.

"It finally sunk in! I simultaneously cried and smiled. This experience has truly given me some solace over the past couple months."

This is only one of three such stories I have heard in which a brief visit by a nurse, who referred to herself as Angel, appeared the day before the passing of a loved one, and was never seen by others.

CHAPTER FIVE
Arousal from Coma

We note from biology that major organ systems shut down as people are dying, but the order of that shutdown varies. The heart may stop first, or the brain may disengage, or the kidneys may stop pumping. As the body deteriorates, the person whom we know and love is still there and may have some residual capacity for communication, which mostly is untapped, since the overwhelming majority of people who experience this shutdown are on their way to the next phase of existence.

But there are a series of narratives that I have recorded from witnesses of such events, which clinically may be examples of "arousal out of coma," but which also may be defined as "terminal lucidity."

∞

Sixty-year-old Jerry visited his mother when her health was in rapid decline. She was living with his sister in another state. He recognized that her remaining time was short, and he desperately wanted to be there and tell her how much he loved her.

"I spent two hours with her on my last afternoon," he told me. "Near the end of my visit, she said 'Father is home! I am home!' I said, 'Yes, Mom, he returned to his home and you are home, too.'"

Jerry left later that afternoon, and was informed that his mom had quietly passed soon after his departure.

∞

A physician friend's father-in-law, an eighty-year-old Polish-American man, had been losing weight, having abdominal pain, and was in an increasingly debilitated condition. The family kept him as comfortable as possible at home, providing love and support. He eventually lapsed into a coma. His extended family convened at the bedside one evening. This is what I was told happened next.

"He became suddenly aroused, opened his eyes, and started clearly speaking names in Polish. My wife immediately recognized the names as those of deceased relatives. Then her father passed."

My colleague shared that the man's first language was Polish, but he had not spoken it in many years. It is a common report about patients with fading cognition. Many, in their last moments, revert to communication in their first language.

∞

Fifty-two-year-old Samantha's mother was dying of Stage 4 lung cancer. "The family was around the bed and with her in a progressively failing state. In an instant, she opened her eyes and started reciting names of deceased relatives — in Czech. She then relaxed and fell asleep. The kids were all scared. But the next morning, amazingly, my mother was able to get out of bed and make breakfast for everybody; although having difficulty standing up, she was smiling all the while. She soon returned to bed and expired three days later."

∞

A sixty-year-old clergyman often visits families of patients who are dying in the hospital, a hospice setting, or at home. Through those experiences he heard four very similar stories, three from concerned people he had known socially, while the fourth came from his mother-in-law, who suffered from a brain tumor and had lapsed into a coma. In each case, he said,

"The strangest thing happened. They aroused, started mumbling, became calm, and died shortly thereafter."

The same pastor learned I was assembling stories that explored the separation between life, death, and perhaps afterlife. He sought me out to share how he and his wife had attended his mother-in-law's last days in an assisted-living facility.

"It was three days before she died due to congestive heart failure and COPD. I had been to the hospital at night and noticed that she was gasping for air. The family went home to sleep. Later, a nurse called to tell us to come as soon as possible. My wife and I found her mother in a hospital bed, sitting up, and noted that she had her eyes wide open and was staring at the opposite wall. She was smiling. She was listing a bunch of names of people I didn't know, but my wife knew them because they were all deceased relatives. My mother-in-law was very excited, and the recitation lasted between maybe five and ten minutes, although I lost track of time. She calmed down, closed her eyes, and fell asleep. For the next three days, she survived, was minimally alert, smiling, and no longer anxious. Ultimately, she closed her eyes and passed."

These last two narratives are unique among my accumulated stories, in that the moments of sudden arousal and final passing were separated by a period of days. In all of the other stories I have compiled or read about, the passing after awakening was immediate.

∞

A retired hospice nurse told me about caring for a fourteen-year-old boy with a fatal brain tumor. One day, she was alone with him in his room. She stated that he opened his eyes and said, "Who are all those people?" Then he smiled, and immediately passed away.

∞

Sixty-nine-year-old Gail, a colleague of mine, sat by her father's bedside in his last days. She reported that he awakened from a deep sleep and told her, "I see Mother at the top of the stairs. I see light at the top of the stairs. She's waiting for me." He repeated that final phrase, smiled, and passed.

∞

Kelli's mother suffered through many years with Alzheimer's. By the end she essentially had no memory, and in the final phase she lapsed into a coma. While at the bedside, Kelli watched her mother open her eyes and say, "I see my son."

"Then my mother passed," Kelli told me. "It occurred to me that my deceased brother had come to take her on."

∞

Seventy-year-old Megan had been serving and supporting her husband for at least six years through which he struggled with multiple conditions, including Alzheimer's. He had been saying strange things, was disoriented, and unable to pay attention to conversation or formulate sentences.

Ultimately, he slipped into a coma. Weeks later, Megan reported this to me:

"I was at his bedside. He was resting peacefully but hardly breathing. He opened his eyes and said, 'I see you, Mom.' I knew he was at peace as he died and so, I was at peace."

∞

Seventy-seven-year-old Peter was a caregiver for a lady for many years. Even after the woman developed Alzheimer's she remained a pleasant, happy, enjoyable person. She would forget what she had said and what she had done, but she was always kind and courteous.

After the lady lapsed into a coma Peter continued to care for her. One day, Peter heard the lady say: "Why is my grandmother coming? I guess I will be there soon." Peter told me that the lady giggled, then smiled, and passed.

∞

Another hospice nurse told me about an extraordinary event regarding a patient she had cared for in the past. It occurred on a hot, humid August day, the air-conditioning at the hospital was not working. A ninety-year-old woman was lying in a coma. The nurse ushered the chaplain into the room to administer the last rights. The chaplain could not help but observe that the windows were closed and the room was stifling hot. At that particular moment, the lady awakened, sat up, and said, "Do you feel the breeze?" She looked toward the window, smiled, laid back, and expired.

∞

A former ICU nurse from Florida, fifty-six-year-old Cathy, told me that she observed numerous patients make comments just before passing, and many had languished in comas before the event. Apparently, many caregivers, especially hospice workers, have witnessed such scenes. Cathy also claimed that the nurses who trained her in intensive care work were familiar with this phenomenon, and witnessed it many times

∞

This unique observation fails to fit into any category, so I have taken the liberty to add it to the final moments grouping. Several years ago, 35-year-old Kara was a bereavement counselor with a local hospice. Frequently, she was called to "death events" to support family members of the dying or deceased patient. One evening on her drive home from the office, she was notified that a patient's death was imminent and that her support was requested. The patient had been diagnosed with Alzheimer's disease and lived in a nursing care facility for many years. When she arrived, the spouse and grandson were sitting at her bedside. The patient was lying in bed with her eyes closed and mouth open. She looked peaceful. But the physical signs of approaching death were evident. Kara looked out the window and saw two crows walking around in the grass. The spouse and grandson expressed their fatigue, so she told them she would sit with the patient for a while. After they left the room, Kara sat for about ten minutes holding the patient's hand. Suddenly, she noticed a very faint, white mist gather above the patient's head. She thought her eyes might be deceiving her. She looked away and when she fixed her eyes at the top of the patient's head, she saw the mist gather again. Within 1-2 minutes, the patient had died. She called the nurse and her spouse back into the room. They sat with the patient a while longer and talked about their lives together. During that time, the electricity to the room flickered several times. The spouse and grandson said they felt the electricity flicker was their loved one saying goodbye.

CHAPTER SIX

Levitation & Near-Death Experiences

This section describes events in which subjects experienced what can be characterized as "traveling away from their bodies".

The feeling or act of leaving one's body and hovering above it is called levitation. Typically, the person perceives the scene without fear or any real emotion, other than amazement that comes with the sight of their own body in a state of distress they no longer feel.

A more profound departure from one's body is often called an out-of-body experience (OBE). In this situation, there is a dissociative sensation of perceiving oneself from an external vantage point, as though the mind or soul has left the body and is acting on its own. These experiences are different from a dream or an insight wherein the object or the idea comes to the recipient.

As noted in the introduction, the categorizations are somewhat informal. Some events could be described as either NDE or OOB or both. Like any experience in which more happens than we can observe or understand, we must rely on subjective interpretation to make any sense of what has happened.

LEVITATIONS

Ronnie, a young vibrant nurse, was having a C-section for a term pregnancy, and while pulling and talking, the doctors could not get the child out through the open abdomen. She was in tremendous pain.

"I saw the anesthesiologist administer an extra dose of intravenous morphine, at which point I went into anaphylactic shock. I rose above my body and saw them rush in the crash cart. I remember giving some of my light to each of the doctors in the room. I eventually wound up in ICU, receiving four pints of blood, but even there I could remember the event."

Ronnie also told me about a second event that occurred during another birth. "I delivered a stillborn baby girl. When I recovered from the gynecologic procedure, the nurse admitted my three-year-old son, Christopher, who had been in the waiting room. He immediately remarked that he had seen baby angels floating up into the sky. He said, 'Mommy, God has taken our baby angel.' This mitigated some of the sorrow and pain which I experienced. Eventually, I did recover completely."

∞

A sixty-two-year-old clergyman recounted a story he had heard in seminary that changed his life. "I was privileged to have a professor of the Old Testament Bible in the seminary training. The man was known to have had a bad heart; in fact, in 1970 he had died on the operating table during a conventional procedure. The professor stated that he levitated and noted that the scene was peaceful. He was looking down dispassionately as he rose up and saw the color blue, which became brighter and more intense. He was eventually resuscitated and jerked back into his body. He told the operating surgeon exactly what he had heard them saying. And he told them, 'Everything is going to be fine.'"

∞

Another clergyman excitedly told me about an unbelievable event recounted by his mother. She was having surgery when she apparently suffered cardiac arrest and was thought to have died. "She levitated and saw me in tears and heard my father's voice, all in an instant. She was told in a soft voice that she should not look up. She understood at that instant that she would travel upwards if she disobeyed. Because she felt encouraged to stay, she did not want to leave."

His mother was jolted back to life on the operating table, although she did not regain consciousness until she was transferred to the recovery room. There, she told the surgeon about her experience and asked what happened and whether she had moved. He told her that she had never moved but her heart had stopped for an instant during surgery and they had to bring her back.

∞

When John was a high school student, he was very despondent about his father's passing. He struggled and eventually left school. When I heard this story, I was quite disturbed and decided to visit him and take him to lunch. On our second get-together, he shared the following story with me:

"I saw myself elevated six feet above the bed, looking down on myself. At that point, I saw my father come through the bedroom door and walk into my room. I saw my physical self get out of bed, and the two of us intensely hugged each other. I asked my dad why he had to leave me. My father responded, 'It was my time to go, and now it is your time to grow up and be a man.' My father disappeared, and I woke up flat in bed, crying. It took me years to understand that magic of the moment."

∞

Forty-two-year-old Donna once ran her station wagon off the road, collided with the abutment of a bridge and was thrown from the car. She felt herself elevated above a badly damaged car, looking down on the scene without much emotion. She observed a truck driver stop and run out to help her. She remembered saying, "I have to come back and help the children." At that point, she abruptly returned back to her body. She ignored her injuries and pain and crawled into the backseat to help pull her two children to safety. Then she collapsed and awoke later in the ambulance.

∞

Alice has a vivid memory from age eight that has stuck with her to this day. "While lying in bed, I began to hover over myself on the ceiling. The ceiling gave me some perspective. I then floated around the house, into my brother's and sister's bedrooms, and over my sleeping parents. I was watching the whole family in the house. After some unmeasurable time, I dropped down into my body in the bed and was unable to move for a while. I was never afraid, just amazed, and I could not understand how this all had happened."

NEAR-DEATH EXPERIENCES

In an NDE, a person experiences the vision or distinct feeling that they are in the process of dying and moving over to a new place. Often, observers report that the person's heart stopped beating, or they lost all measurable responsiveness. The person's consciousness persists, however, often through a strange floating sensation, and he or she does not feel pain or despair, only wonderment and perhaps confusion.

∞

Many years ago, the wife of a colleague, fifty-six-year-old Syd, told me a story about her father. He had been an Argentinian businessman and quite shrewd and meticulous in his work. He suffered a heart attack and survived after being resuscitated. When he returned, Syd said he was a very different person, much happier and more generous. He spent the rest of his life helping others and contributing to charities and to the pleasure of his friends and family.

∞

Seventy-one-year-old Mary, while visiting Greece, and always gone to church on Sundays. While speaking to the priest after one particular mass, she delved into some deeper spiritual subjects. The priest then shared his own personal experience. As a younger man, he had experienced cardiac arrest and felt that he left his body. He travelled through a tunnel, and he told her that he visited the Garden of Angels. He was told that it was not his time, and he had to go back. He said he came back with a rush. He told Mary that this incident is what motivated him to join the priesthood.

∞

In 1983, a mechanical specialist was fixing a surgical microscope I used in my practice. As we chatted, he made a reference to an accident that had happened. When I asked him about the situation, he opened up to me:

"I was in an automobile accident several years ago. I levitated above and watched my body being extracted from the car by the EMTs. I saw myself being loaded into the ambulance, all without any real emotion – just observing. As I levitated, the sky above me became bluer, nicer, and there was accompanying music. I remember going through a tunnel, and I met my deceased grandmother. She said to me, 'It is not your time yet, you have to go back.' Boom! I awoke in ICU after ten days in a coma. Those ten days seemed like twenty seconds to me."

∞

A number of years ago, I happened to examine sixty-year-old Carla three days after she had an NDE. She didn't feel like talking about it in detail, but she did say, "I went through a tunnel. I didn't know what was happening, and someone told me it was not my time yet." There was more to her vision, but acknowledging those details was enough of a testament for her. Not everyone is ready to share of these experiences, at least early on.

∞

I was walking through the emergency room entrance of my hospital one Saturday afternoon. As I passed by an open room, I was drawn to the commotion created by two doctors and a nurse trying to revive a woman named Millie, whom I have known for years as a patient. She apparently had a cardiac arrest. Within seconds, she was given electric shocks and woke up. She gasped for air but quickly began to breathe freely.

I was immobilized watching the scene. Then she turned her head and stared at me and said, "What the hell are you doing here?" I just walked on and let the appropriate physicians take care of her. Although I naturally was curious to know what had happened to her, I figured I would learn more if I waited for her to stabilize.

And I stayed in the hospital for about an hour, visiting a friend who was recovering from gallbladder surgery. Eventually, I was allowed to visit Millie in the ICU, where she had been taken for follow-up care.

She was alert, sitting up in bed, and she immediately recognized me. Here is how she recalled the event:

"I went to the hospital with chest pain. I received immediate attention as the pain increased. I started to pass out and the last thing I heard was an intern saying, 'I think she is going.' The next thing I recall is floating upward over the scene, quite relaxed, although the scene below looked quite chaotic. It got bluer and nice, with lovely music. Next, I found myself at the foot of a tall individual with sandals. I thought it was Jesus and I said, 'I have to go back because Herbie and the kids need me.'"

Millie was fifty-eight at the time. I was grateful to have witnessed her experience in some small way.

∞

This and the next incident are examples in which a relative or friend is sharing the out-of-body experiences of someone else.

DB had a fifty-year-old friend who owned a bar in a small Maryland town. He shared the following story with me:

"One evening, my friend threw a disruptive drunk out. Two days later, while he was cleaning up alone in the back of the bar, the man came in and hit him in the head with a wrench. As he did not return home, his wife came looking for him early in the morning and found him unconscious in a pool of blood. She called the EMTs, and he was thought to be dead.

"His body was being driven away to a funeral home when he suddenly woke up. Later on, my friend said that he had taken a trip up in the air to some very pleasant place with happy people. He explained that he did not have a care in the world and had no pain. Then, suddenly he dropped back down with a bang in some vehicle (probably the ambulance). As it turned out, he both survived and saw his attacker put in prison for this incident and previous offences."

∞

Sixty-five-year-old Daphne shared a story from twenty-five years ago. "When I was in a medical center having my daughter, I contracted what was later diagnosed as a strep infection in the hospital delivery room. It was during the years when women were sent home twenty-four hours after giving birth, but in my case, it turned out to be a terrible decision to leave the hospital so early.

"Traveling to our home on an island, I saw a tiny sign that read, 'If in need, call the sheriff.' I remember thinking that I had never seen that little sign before and, as our remote location did not have an active 911 emergency contact, it was a good thing to know.

"Later in the day, about forty-two hours after the baby's delivery, I became very ill. The OB/GYN on call at the medical center dismissed my symptoms and advised me to take a warm bath. My husband was not concerned until he saw three deer come to the bedroom window and peer in. He advised me that this was bad news: a group of deer such as we witnessed was a harbinger of death. Anyway, it prompted me to call the sheriff.

"The sheriff's office called an ambulance, which arrived shortly thereafter. They took me out of the house on a stretcher, careful to navigate around the deer, who hadn't budged. In the ambulance were the driver, an EMT doctor, and my neighbor, a retired M.D. His wife, a retired nurse, stayed with the newborn while we were on our way to the nearest hospital.

"The next part is rather dreamy. I was shaking so hard that it felt like I was being strapped down, and then I felt like I was being put on a toboggan just as I heard the physician say, 'There is no pulse.' It seemed as if I was pushed out of the back of the ambulance into an ice tunnel. It was a bumpy ride, and the surroundings were shadowy and in black and white. I reached the end of something, and the straps of the toboggan were released. I saw a billowy figure four feet in front of me. He was dressed in a white robe, but there was so much light in back of him that the robe looked like it was merely iridescent. Initially, I thought it was Jesus, but it was my (deceased) father, and I was really so happy to see him looking so well. He said, 'I am proud of you, darling.' He then smiled and disappeared."

She then received appropriate antibiotic therapy and recovered.

∞

Thirty-two-years-old Wendy shared this dramatic account with me:

"Approximately 10:30 a.m. one morning, I was traveling on Route 26 south and was headed down a deep curve in the road. My car hit wet leaves and an oil residue and crossed the

76

center line directly in the path of a Mack truck which was fully loaded with logs. Apparently with the head-on crash, I lost consciousness and sustained many injuries.

"I awoke when I was wheeled through the ER doors and heard them yell: 'This guy is gone. He is gone. Code blue. Code blue.'

"Suddenly the pain was gone. It was replaced with bliss. I knew what they were saying about me. I had worked during my early years behind a desk in a medical facility and I knew when a patient stopped breathing in the hospital, they called the code blue phone. I knew that I was dead, but it was the most wonderful feeling that I have ever experienced in my life, before and since. My eyesight was hampered due to the blood covering my eyes, but I could look down and see the doctor and nurse working on my lifeless body. Then my vision became clearer than my usual eyesight. I was out-of-body and above everyone, looking down at the body, seeing the organized chaos, and I didn't care. Everything was wonderful.

"As the moment or seconds went by, I began slowly to turn away from the scene and head in some unknown direction that took me behind the scenes in the ER room. But I was gently nudged back by something that made me face the scene, and something in my head said, 'Not yet.'

Then all of a sudden, I noticed that I was back in my body and could not 'see' anything — and the pain was back. I felt that God had intervened. It took months before I finally fully recovered, but I never forgot this amazing experience, which changed my life."

∞

Forty-year-old Evie shared with me an amazing experience from early in her life:

"It all started while I was in my twenties and during my fourth pregnancy. It was the evening on Easter when I began to wash clothes in my bathtub. Suddenly, I felt something was wrong with my unborn child. I started to feel contractions and began to bleed, so I immediately called my brother and asked him to take me to the hospital.

"When I arrived, the medical staff rushed me to a room and used a baby monitor which enabled them to hear my baby's heartbeat. After a few hours had passed, they sent me home, and I was told that everything was fine. The next morning, I felt something inside of my body drop, and I noticed that I was bleeding heavily. I called 911 and was rushed back to the hospital. About three hours later, the nurse stepped out of the room and returned with the doctor. They informed me that I had lost part of the placenta and that my baby's heartbeat could no longer be found. Nine hours later, I had given birth to my stillborn baby.

"During the birth, I started to feel weak and my eyes began to feel heavy. The nurse kept telling me to stay awake, so I tried my best to do so. The next thing I remember is me seeing my body lying on a bed with doctors and nurses surrounding me. After looking at my surroundings, I realized I had passed away because my body felt like it was as light as air. I was then in a white clouded area, and I could barely see anything in front of me. I screamed out to God: 'God, no! No, this can't be! I have to be there for my children because they need me!' I then felt God put His hand on my forehead. He then told me to go be with my children as He pushed me away. I could feel my body falling and when it stopped, I immediately woke up, or so I thought.

"Little did I know that I had been in the morgue with a sheet over my head. My doctor had been so contrite that he ran down and listened to my heart with a stethoscope. He thought that he heard a faint heartbeat and demanded that they take me back to the ICU.

"I had been put on life support and remained in the hospital. My bodiless experience seemed to have taken seconds, but I was informed that I had been in the ICU for three weeks. Later, when I was taken off life support, I began to have asthma attacks.

"Some years later, I was stricken with another asthma attack which caused me to code. The second time, I was amongst the clouds and I noticed a light in the distance. I spoke with God and told Him that my kids still needed me. God then said to me in a calm soft tone, 'This is your last chance.' God then put His hand on my forehead and pushed me back to my body. When I woke up, I saw that I was connected to machines which were breathing for me. I am appreciative that God had given me a second chance at life."

∞

This is a very different NDE because the reporter was not the person who died and returned. In fact, the return of the deceased appeared to yet a third person in a dream. However, this story is so valuable because it sheds light on the possibility of choice while out of body.

Eighty-four-year-old Sarah shared with me one of the most remarkable stories that I have recorded. The younger of her two daughters died two days before her fortieth birthday. "She was a lively redhead with a frivolous sense of humor and had always been someone who was larger than life. And my two daughters were the best of friends.

One or two months after my daughter passed, my older daughter, Susan, envisioned her sister in a dream, which she described as a visitation. Susan asked her sister in that dream: "What have you been doing?"

Sarah, the mother, related the rest of the story. "My younger daughter reported that she had originally hung over her own body but felt no pain, in fact experienced great relief. She then hovered around the house she shared with her boyfriend of the past ten years. At that point, she visited my older daughter to ask if she wanted to join her for some fun. Susan was so delighted to see her sister that she immediately agreed. The two of them then flew to a Rolls Royce agency and jumped into a Silver Shadow Rolls Royce convertible. Instantaneously they were flying through the air, sharing jokes, conversing, laughing, and enjoying a great time together.

Susan fully understood that this was occurring in a dream, but it felt so real to her. As the Rolls Royce was flying over the Rockies, her sister revealed that she had been given a choice about returning to earth or staying where she was. She stated that she had chosen to stay. Immediately, Susan became upset and angry by that decision. At that point, the ride and visitation abruptly ended, and Susan awoke from the dream."

Sarah concluded that Susan felt differently by the next day and realized that her sister was very happy with her choice. After this apocryphal experience was shared, Sarah's whole family felt comforted and gained some solace regarding the loss.

CHAPTER SEVEN

Renowned Near-Death Experiences

The earliest cave dwellers, civilizations, and religions have struggled to deal with the existential question of death; in doing so, they created their own descriptions and contours of an afterlife.

Homer, Virgil, and Dante provided graphic descriptions of the boundary between life and death. The Roman philosopher, Lucretius, explored reality and understood that all things were composed of atoms, the world was round, and time and space were infinite. In his cosmology, what came after death was a matter of fate. Lucretius in *The Nature of*

Things wrote extensively about happiness and discredited the fear of death.

Many celebrities and writers, having experienced near death, have felt compelled to advance awareness about the phenomena and to provide an alternative to the impression of the soul's finality after death. What follows are a few well known accounts of descriptive NDEs.

∞

Ernest Hemingway described a near-death experience after being hit with shrapnel near Piave in northern Italy during World war I[1]:

"A big Austrian trench mortar bomb of the type that used to be called ash cans exploded in the darkness. I died then. I felt my soul or something coming right out of my body, like you'd pull a silk handkerchief out of a pocket by one corner. It flew around and then came back and went in again and I wasn't dead anymore."

Hemingway remained deeply affected by this out-of-body experience, and was never again as "hard-boiled" as he once had been. *A Farewell to Arms* contains a passage where one character, Frederic Henry, undergoes the same confrontation with death that Hemingway did.

∞

---

[1] Death Experiences-Awaken as seen on YouTube 11/15/2019

In March 1961, at the age of 33, the actress Elizabeth Taylor suffered a respiratory arrest. She stated in an interview with Oprah Winfrey[2] that she had seen the tunnel. "I was pronounced dead four times and had no vital signs for five minutes. I was not afraid of dying at that point. There were people all around me as I floated into this tunnel. bright sun, and warmth, and it was wonderful. I saw lots of figures. And Mike Todd (her previous husband, said to be her true love) was there and I was still mourning him. He said, 'Elizabeth, it is not your time yet. Force yourself to go back. You have to fight to go back, baby.'" She said that she wanted to stay but had to return. When she started to wake up, she immediately shared her experience with all eleven doctors in the room, so later on she wouldn't think she was crazy. Elizabeth stated "I had been pronounced dead and my obituary had already appeared in the paper. I never had such good reviews. I never talked about it for years, then I started reading about other people having the same experience, and I felt inclined to tell mine."

∞

Clint Walker, better known as "Cheyenne" in the sixties television western, suffered a heart attack and cardiac arrest at the age of forty-four after a skiing accident in which a ski

---

[2] Elizabeth Taylor appeared on the "Oprah Winfrey Show" on March 4th, 1992.

pole punctured his heart. He stated that he had gone up and seen what the other side looked like, and it changed him and his views about the finality of death. In his description of the event he said, "I was out of my body...into my spirit body. I became more alive, more alert, and more aware. That spirit body had no aches or pains. I am not all that concerned about going back. There must be something that I still need to do."[3]

Clint shared that while he was out-of-body, he was declared dead by two heart specialists. But a third heart specialist thought that he might be alive and intervened. After he recovered, he strongly felt the need to share his experience about a realm beyond death. He no longer thought of death as terminal.

∞

Jane Seymour was making the biopic on Maria Callas in Spain when she came down with bronchitis. During treatment she received an antibiotic injection accidentally into a vein instead of a muscle, suffering anaphylactic shock. She shared in an interview how her subsequent experience changed her outlook and approach to life.

---

[3] Clint Walker, Television Academy Interviews, 11/6/2012

"The nurse that had administered [the antibiotic] saved my life by injecting me with cortisone and adrenaline, but I did actually leave my body, see the white light, see the people resuscitating me, and all of that. And after that, I realized that you take nothing with you in this life."

After a pause she added, "It was a wonderful moment really. It made me realize how simple it is. It's all about living and being loved. End of story – and the difference you may have made along the way. It simplified things for me. It stopped me from worrying about dying or death or anything like that. I realized there's no pain or panic attached. Your life is incredibly worth living, and I don't want to waste a moment of it."[4]

∞

During filmmaker George Lucas' senior year in high school, he suffered a horrible car accident which almost took his life. He told Oprah Winfrey about how the accident made him reevaluate his life and conclude that every day is a bonus.[5]

"When I was eighteen, I was in an automobile accident and went through a near-death experience. I was actually

---

[4] Desert News Malibu California 8/22/08

[5] George Lucas appeared on the "Oprah: Next Chapter" program on the OWN network on January 22, 2012.

taken away from the scene, presumed dead, and it wasn't until I reached the hospital that the doctors revived my heartbeat and brought me back to life. This is the kind of experience that molds peoples' beliefs. But I have found that most of my conclusions have evolved from observing life since that time. If I've come to know anything, it is that these questions are as unknowable for us as they would be for a tree or for an ant."

∞

In 1964, during Peter Sellers' first in a rapid series of eight heart attacks, his heart stopped, and he was declared dead. He reported to Shirley MacLaine that he had an out-of-body experience and saw the bright loving light. Sellers stated, "Well, I felt myself leave my body. I just floated out of my physical form, and I saw them cart my body away to the hospital. I went with it...I wasn't frightened or anything like that because I was fine; and it was my body that was in trouble."[6]

The doctor saw that Sellers was dead but massaged his heart vigorously. Meanwhile, "I looked around myself and I saw an incredibly beautiful bright loving white light above me. I wanted to go to that white light more than anything. I've never wanted anything more. I know there was love, real

---

[6] *Out on a Limb* by Shirley MacLaine Bantam Books 1983

love, on the other side of the light which was attracting me so much. It was kind and loving, and I remember thinking, 'That's God.'"

Peter's out-of-body soul tried to elevate toward the light, but he fell short. "Then I saw a hand reach through the light. I tried to touch it, to grab onto it, to clasp it so it could sweep me up and pull me through it." But Sellers' heart began beating again, and at that instant, the hand's voice said, "It's not time. Go back and finish. It's not time." As the hand receded, Sellers felt himself floating back down to his body, waking up bitterly disappointed.

∞

Dr. Raymond Moody[7] suffered a cardiac arrest after a medication incident; the following recollection of a "separation" and seeing "spirit guides" is attributed to him.

"I could feel the ambulance accelerate, hitting speed bumps hard as we headed to the hospital. An elephant was sitting on my chest. My eyes were closed, or at least I think they were. Either way, I could see nothing. My heart stopped. What happened next is almost indescribable, but I will do my best to make it less so. I could feel myself separate from the world around me. In a funny way, it was almost like cellophane being pulled off a smooth surface, one reality

---

[7] *Paranormal: My Life in Pursuit of the Afterlife* by Dr Moody

separating from another. I sensed spirits around me, helpful presences, who were there to guide me through this separation. I tried to see these spirit guides, but I could not make them out because I was surrounded by a light that was not of this world. I could hear them speaking, and although I couldn't make out what was being said, their presence was soothing and calm. I felt a radiant love from them. I felt myself 'start up' again as the doctors pumped my stomach and gave me a shot of a stimulant to the heart. The light went away, the spirits were there no more, and I came to in the emergency room."

Dr. Moody was willing to discuss his experience because he felt it was so integral to living a complete life. Since it happened, he has written and lectured extensively on the subject of life after death.

∞

Neurosurgeon Eben Alexander, M.D.[8], who wrote *Proof of Heaven*, went into a coma for a week due to an untreatable brain infection. He was put on a ventilator, and the family and doctors were about to remove all life support when he suddenly awoke. He later shared a description of his out-of-body experience.

---

[8] www.ebanalexander.com

"My coma taught me many things. First and foremost, near-death experiences and related mystical states of awareness reveal crucial truths about the nature of existence. Simply dismissing them as hallucinations is convenient for many in the conventional scientific community but only continues to lead them away from the deeper truth these experiences are revealing to us. The conventional reductive materialist (physicalist) model embraced by many in the scientific community, including its assumption that the physical brain creates consciousness and that our human existence is birth-to-death and nothing more, is fundamentally flawed. At its core, that physicalist model intentionally ignores what I believe is the fundament of all existence—consciousness itself."

∞

The world-renowned psychiatrist, Carl G. Jung, while hospitalized for a broken leg suffered a heart attack. During the time he had no heartbeat or pulse, he experienced a near-death experience. He later wrote, "My nurse afterwards told me it was as if I was surrounded by a bright glow."[9] His vivid encounter with the light, plus the intensely meaningful insights, led Jung to conclude that his experience came from something real and eternal.

---

[9] Jung's Remembrances Hermetik International, Hermetik Academy

Jung's experience was unique in that he remembered himself floating a thousand miles above the earth. Additionally, he experienced numerous other events which could not be explained through accepted reality. His story is one of many in which a person devotes the remainder of their lifetime to analyzing the question of death as it pertains to life. His writings are extensive, and in a 1959 BBC interview he professed his belief in God.

∞

In 1943 at the age of twenty, George G. Ritchie, Jr. was a private in the army stationed in Texas, awaiting a transfer to Richmond's Medical College of Virginia, where he would train to become a doctor for the military. In his book, *Return to Tomorrow*, he wrote that he contracted pneumonia and suffered a cardiopulmonary arrest[10]. The army physician in charge found no evidence of respiration or cardiac impulse and declared Ritchie dead.

Ritchie reported that during this moment, he left his body. At first, he wandered around the hospital ward, unaware he was dead. He found it strange no one could see him. He returned to his room and recognized his lifeless body, which had been covered with a sheet and his fraternity ring. The room then became bright, and Ritchie found

---

[10] Hampton Roads Publishing 5/1/15

himself in the presence of a being he presumed was Jesus, who guided him through several realms of the afterlife before Ritchie was told to return to his body.

As the hospital attendant was preparing Ritchie's body for the morgue, he thought he detected movement in Ritchie's chest and called for a medical officer. The physician promptly administered a shot of adrenaline into his heart, which restored his breath and heartbeat. Ritchie then returned to life transformed by his profound near-death experience, and he spent his medical career studying the subject.

∞

Pim von Lommel, M.D., a Dutch cardiologist, reported in *Consciousness Beyond Life* that prior to the advent of cardiac defibrillation, patients who suffered a cardiac arrest (the heart stops beating) always died. However, the introduction of the electronic stimulator in 1967 brought many pulseless patients back to life. Dr. von Lommel related how his first recovering cardiac arrest patient gave him an enthusiastic description of an out-of-body experience. Subsequently, a dozen of the next fifty revived patients gave a remarkably similar description of their encounters. And they became more social and compassionate.

In 2002, Von Lommel and some fellow researchers published a study on near-death experiences in the renowned medical journal, *The Lancet*[11]. The NDE, Von Lommel argued, "cannot be attributed to imagination, psychosis, or oxygen deprivation." He also reported that after such profound experiences, patients' personalities often underwent a permanent change.

People who do not have such a dramatic encounter as a NDE may experience a change in their life view as well. In this regard, Scott Wright and colleagues published *The Impact of Dreams of the Deceased on Bereavement: A Survey of Hospital Care Givers*[12]. The authors surveyed 278 grieving individuals regarding the relationship between their dreams and the mourning process. Fifty-eight percent of respondents reported dreams of the deceased with varying levels of frequency; sixty percent of the participants felt that the dreams reduced the depth of their grieving.

Many of these noteworthy people who experienced their NDE have made it their life's work to publish and disseminate their stories. In contradistinction *Is Death Really*

---

[11] The Lancet, June 15, 2002

[12] Published 2/28/13 in PubMed

a Mystery? brings to light the extraordinary accounts of ordinary people who will never otherwise tell their stories. My reporters have never published their unique experiences but have them privately embedded in their memories. They have used their encounters to reevaluate their beliefs about death and to enhance their lives.

In the next chapter I will share some of my own formative experiences, which have contributed to my writing *Is Death Really A Mystery?* These occurrences actually began before my déjà vu experience at age nine, which was the subject of the prologue. Many of my recollections and memories could well fit into the previous categories.

CHAPTER EIGHT

My Personal Journey

Only in retrospect, do we gain comprehension. As Søren Kierkegaard stated: "Life can only be understood backwards; but it must be lived forwards." As I look back on previous experiences, their importance seems so obvious. But in fact, we can't understand many events until we encounter a similar situation or experience later in life.

As someone who had been found to be dyslexic or having ADD, I nearly failed third grade. My parents were advised if I was unable to read in the last two months that I would have to repeat the grade with the same teacher. Fortunately for me, I realized that I could memorize the assignments and thus passed.

Despite the elementary school's principal's opinion that I was unlikely to graduate high school, my fifth-grade teacher had confidence in me and understood my potential. I finally caught up to the advanced classes by tenth grade. However, I still had to memorize four thousand words for the English College Board Exam in order to compensate for the time required for reading comprehension. Incidentally, I never encountered the subject of learning disabilities until I became an ophthalmologist. In retrospect, I now realize that dyslexia allowed me to understand things outside conventional borders.

My first memory is of nearly drowning as a nine-month-old. I remember being underwater, looking up and being relatively unfazed by it all. Almost immediately, my mother jumped in and pulled me out of the water.

I have other early childhood memories which are less consequential. However, I began recalling my dreams around the age of five. One particularly recurrent and terrifying dream featured my crossing a railroad trestle over a deep gorge. Midway across the bridge, an oncoming train would always be bearing down on me. Since I could never outrun the train, I would climb down and hold onto one of the slats beneath the rails. But the train never ended. As I became exhausted, I would finally let go and fall to what I presumed to be my death. Yet I never did die. I always awoke suddenly before hitting the rocks below.

This was frightening for a little kid, and the dream repeated enough times that I came to dread encountering it again when I went to bed. It extended into months of torture. Finally, during yet another dream, I decided that, since I had never actually died, I would just jump as soon as the train approached. That's what I did and that was the last time I had that dream.

Two events in childhood taught me to be more compassionate. One was a short-term eye injury at age eleven, which introduced me to pain and how a doctor may not listen to a patient. The other was after my grandfather's stroke when he moved into my bedroom for three years. Not only did I help take care of him, I taught him to play first base with me and the rest of the kids.

College, in a liberal arts environment, was enlightening and encouraged discovery. It provided an integration of the sciences and the humanities, demanding being fully responsible for time management. I had the opportunity to learn two languages while being a biology major.

Medical school was a horse of an entirely different color. You were expected to memorize and reflexively regurgitate information. Examinations were multiple choice – you were either right or wrong. Memorizing 30,000 new words is an arduous process. Nonetheless, it taught the scientific methods and the tools of objective examination. At the same time, you became involved in other people's lives. These two very different educational experiences provided the impetus and ability to navigate two very different levels of comprehension.

Throughout my early adulthood, and maybe extending all the way back to my nine-year-old leap above the crevasse, I wondered about the purpose of life. I realized that death was inevitable and an essential part of our journey. I read with great interest the books that described NDEs and wondered how these compelling stories might correlate with what I knew and what was accepted by conventional wisdom. I had come to realize the brain is a prisoner of the five senses, and there was something beyond the realm of logic and consciousness. I had periodic déjà vu experiences and realized that they represented scenes beyond the present moment.

My parents were not convinced of the idea of life after death. My mother was particularly skeptical by the lack of empirical evidence. However, four nights before my mother's eventual death, she had a profound and reassuring dream. The next morning, when I came to see her, she shared, "I know what you were talking about and I saw the other side. I am now ready to go."

My father, who did not believe in any other side, called me ecstatically one month after my mother's passing. "Rob," he said. "You won't believe what happened last night. I was in this dream and danced with your mother. I held her close, smelled her fragrance, and touched her hair. I said, 'Ruth, you're wearing purple, a color which you never liked before.' She responded, 'It doesn't matter here anymore,' smiled, and disappeared."

Seven weeks after my father's death, I saw him quite vividly in a dream. I was at a cancer hospital in Philadelphia, trying to get in, but every door was locked. As I approached the last door, I looked to my left. Perhaps twenty-five feet away was my father — smiling, looking young and healthy — telling me, "I'm not in there anymore. I don't have cancer." Dressed casually in his sports clothes, he smiled one last time and disappeared.

One time, my father appeared and told me that I was going to have a hernia and would require a repair. I have always been a devotee of regular exercise and, although three generations of my family had developed hernias, I never had any symptoms. But two days after the dream, a small, right-sided hernia appeared when I was in the shower.

In another dream, I was giving a lecture in a second-floor classroom to a group of undergraduates at my university. I was explaining that we are all connected in this world, although it was far from obvious. My father appeared above and to my left, tanned face, slick-backed hair, wearing a blue suit and looking forty years old. He smiled and raised both hands. Silver threads extended from his fingertips and went towards each student. I said, "See. That's what I was talking about." Dad vanished and the dream ended. I awoke with a big smile.

I have seen my mother many times, perhaps more than thirty. In a remarkable dream, I was looking down on my childhood neighborhood and saw my mother walking on the sidewalk in the shopping center. I zoomed down and walked next to her. "Mom," I said. "What are you doing here?"

"I am going to a celebration," she said.

"Can I come with you?"

"Sure."

So, we walked silently together, down the sidewalk and into the hair salon which she had frequented. She sat down in one of the chairs underneath one of the big hair blower domes, as she spoke to Michael, her hairdresser. I had not seen or said his name in over forty years. I watched them talking for some period of time. Then, abruptly, I found we were walking down a side street and, just as suddenly, we landed inside a three-story Victorian house. My mother and I walked up the steps to the third floor, which was a little dark and dingy. From down the hall, a pale figure came through the door and approached my mother. She and the figure immediately disappeared up and to the right, almost like wisps of smoke. I understood implicitly that the figure was someone who had just died, and my mother was there to take her on.

After I woke, I found out from a friend that my children's piano teacher had passed at 2:00 a.m. that same morning. She was a very dear person with very little family, and my mother had always felt particularly close to her.

I have had a number of dreams in which images, rather than people, were the subjects. In one such dream, I was swimming in a mangrove swamp with two large snakes, one on each side of me. I knew the caduceus, the symbol of medicine, features two snakes winding around a rod. One of the snakes symbolizes art or intuition, the other science or logic. I recognized while in the dream that the snakes conveyed a sort of wisdom and there was no need for me to be frightened. I continued swimming with them.

In another dream, I was at a business meeting. After it broke up, four attendees, who were driving black cars, went to the end of the road and took a left to go home. I was driving a light-colored car and took a right. It indicated to me that I was on a different track or, as some may say, was a little bit different. I drove up a winding road which I had never traveled on previously. On the left at the top of the hill stood a gated house. In fact, the gate was about twenty-five feet high. I could see through the spikes and identify a field in the distance, with horses and a couple of barns to the left. On the right, there was a large, white house and a well-tailored property.

I thought nothing more about this dream until approximately fifteen years later. I was invited to a dinner party by a colleague, whose home I recognized at once as the very same house I had visited in a dream; never knowing that I would find myself there one day, fully awake.

Once, in New York City, I was suffering from an upper respiratory infection and had taken some non-prescription cold medication. I was walking through the Penn Station terminal and feeling a little strange: I was fully conscious and yet my normally sharp perception was hazy. As I walked from one section to the next, I found myself floating about eight feet above myself, looking down on my moving body. I had the sensation that my 'upper self' went through the concrete wall, while my 'lower self' kept walking through the archway and continued on the other side. Shortly thereafter, I returned to myself. I thought, "boy that was weird." Little did I know how this could happen nor could I understand it at the time.

I witnessed a terminal lucidity (coming out of a coma near the end of life) event when I visited the advanced care section at a local retirement home. I had come to pay my respects to a long-time patient who was in the process of dying. When I arrived, there was a nurse in the room and the lady's two daughters were at the foot of the bed. She was lying slightly elevated in bed with her eyes closed. I chatted with the two daughters and then suddenly, the lady opened her eyes, looked above the daughters' heads and said, "Mother." The daughters responded, "It is not Mother. It is your daughters, X and Y." She smiled and passed. Afterwards, I asked the nurse and the other head nurse in the health center if they had witnessed occurrences like this before. They each confirmed they had, at least once before.

Throughout my journey, I have been able to integrate my clinical, academic, and complementary medicine selves. I have tried to teach my patients and readers to become their own medical detectives. Sometimes I'm Sherlock Holmes and sometimes I'm Doctor Watson, but I always look to discover.

CHAPTER NINE
Death & Healing

You have now read these extraordinary accounts of extraordinary occurrences from ordinary people.

But when I embarked on this project, I had been unable to detect any unifying thread to connect these various images and interactions. Any system seemed inadequate as an explanation for so wide a variety of individual experiences. Yet these examples of one of the existential mysteries of human existence seemed so relevant and appeared to indicate that there is an alternate reality.

Eventually I realized that these personal accounts, although individually specific, when grouped together, revealed the following characteristics:

- They were unsolicited, unanticipated, unexplained, and sometimes uncomfortable, but always conveyed meaning.

- They happened to ordinary people who were confronting death and loss.

- The vehicle of these interactions, whether we call it energy, vibration, consciousness, or soul, enabled an undeniable presence that recipients experienced as real.

- Whether receiving visits from loved ones or the feeling of leaving their bodies, people found the experiences conveyed reassurance and positive feelings.

- Most respondents savored their experiences and longed to remain in their dreams. This was also true of those who had near-death encounters before abruptly returning to the earthly plane.

- People were relieved to learn that they were not alone. Many specifically mentioned how these visitations and experiences brought were both happy and comforting. Those still mourning experienced a subsequent reduction in their grieving.

- Those who sensed that they had traveled beyond their bodies report remarkably comparable sensations, often in similar constructions, such as being "surrounded by light;" "I was more aware, more alert, and had better vision;" "I knew that I wasn't dead, and it was the most wonderful feeling."

- Time in both dreams and out of body travels seemed to be irrelevant or, more accurately, just ceased to exist. Space seems to be unlimited, or without observable borders. These encounters cannot be explained through our five senses.

- Déjà vu is the most common clue that this is not the only reality. When we recognize that we could not have possibly been with the same cast of characters and location before, it provides an insight to the limitation of our ability to understand the big picture.

- Despite the similarities, every experience is unique. Only the person who lives it can decipher any messages and decide whether sharing it may provide value to others.

- In contradistinction to people's usual ability to retain an intact memory, most of these individuals were able to vividly recollect their experiences even years_later.

So, how do you interpret these stories? Do you call them "real", or are they figments of imagination? Although difficult to categorize and comprehend, can they be discarded or relegated to fiction?

Each experience can be considered to be an anecdote or a tall tale. However, when similar such anecdotes are collected, they can form a hypothesis. And with enough repetition and confluence, they strongly indicate a reality of their own. In this regard I cannot deny the existence of extracorporeal life, or a soul. It brings comfort to consider (or for those who have experienced it, to believe) that shedding our bodies does not mean our lives end in oblivion. Rather, these encounters strongly indicate a continuity of ourselves in other realms. Thus, these accounts may reduce the angst around dying and the finality of death.

Whatever we believe, we remain at a loss to explain these extraordinary occurrences. Perhaps we should not even try. However, the memories and the specific details of all these experiences are indelible and remain vibrant decades after the event.

These accounts portray that human experience is more than a finite life-to-death drama. But without context and confirmation from others, we might not have the means to treat these experiences as anything more than delusions or pleasant ideations. By sharing their accounts, the people who spoke with me helped me expand my sense of the world, and they may have helped others in a similar way. Writing this book has been such a positive education for me.

As detailed in chapter six, the deceased sister, in declining to return from an NDE, indicated that there may be the opportunity for choice. Just as we have choices in our daily decision making. And in two of the reports, the deceased clearly informed the dreamers that they could communicate when necessary. In two of my childhood frightening dreams I was actually able to alter the outcomes. These and other first-hand reports seem to indicate that there are multiple portals to other existences.

So, is consciousness solely the product of our brain activity, as many mainstream scientists and physicians posit; or is it a non-physical entity (vehicle, spirit, soul) that is able to transcend the body? If consciousness only resides in the brain, how can people levitate, glide away in dreams, and have NDEs, yet retain clear, precise, visual, and auditory memories of their travels?

Neurosurgeon Eben Alexander felt that consciousness is the basis of all existence. Jung called that which is real, eternal and never dies is the soul. Furthermore, he repeatedly wrote that the soul never dies. Perhaps we can say that our souls and our consciousness are one and the same and exist both inside and beyond the brain.

I believe these missing links recorded in this book add to the growing scientific literature that documents that consciousness is, indeed, independent of our bodies. How could someone look down on his or her body during a cardiac arrest or life-threatening surgery, feel no pain, experience happiness, see other entities clearly, return to their body, continue their earthly journey and remember it forever?

Although as adults we no longer routinely perceive Wordsworth's intimations of immortality, we may, on rare and unexpected occasions, be gifted with random flashes. These unanticipated glimpses lift the veil concealing parallel realities, and reveal the ongoing connection to those who have passed. If there is a common thread that connects all of these interactions, it is not dreams, sights, travels, or imagery. I believe it is LOVE.

Let me repeat what Jane Seymour said in her Desert News interview. "It (the NDE) made me realize how simple it is. It's all about living and being loved. End of story – and the difference you may have made along the way. It simplified things for me."

So, is not love the thread that connects and courses through these various stories? Is not love the core need and foundation of humanity? We are all connected and our job is to help one another. Knowledge of these extraordinary encounters can instill greater purpose and meaning in our lives. These many missing links are real and should offer comfort, reframe mourning, and allay the fear of an absolute termination of life. The existential quandary of death should no longer be such a mystery and a shackle on our daily lives.

Learning to perceive what we cannot see is the real mystery which confronts and rewards each of us.

∞   ∞   ∞

RECOMMENDED READING

Many Lives Many Masters by Brian Weiss

The Search for a Soul: Taylor Caldwell's Psychic Lives by Jeff Strearn

Life After Life by Raymond Moody Jr

Sleeping Dreaming Dying by The Dalai Lama & Francisco Varella

Proof of Heaven by Eben Alexander

Life After Death by Carl Gustav Jung

Return from Tomorrow by George Richie

Consciousness Beyond Life by Pim von Lommel

Being Mortal by Atul Gaewande

The Presence of the Absence by Carlos Sluzki

Surviving Death: A Journalist Investigates Evidence for an Afterlife by Leslie Kean

When Breath Becomes Air by Paul Kalamithi

Big Dreams by Kelly Bulkeley

The Unanswered Question: Death, Near Death and the Afterlife by Kurt Lelan

Made in the USA
Monee, IL
28 December 2020